HUEMOTION

Edited by

Joseph A Jalloh
Joe Ahmed
Morrison Jusu

Sierra Leonean Writers Series

Huemotion

Copyright © 2017
Edited by
Joseph A Jalloh, Joe Ahmed & Morrison Jusu

ISBN: 978-9988-8742-0-9

Sierra Leonean Writers Series

Warima/Freetown/Accra
120 Kissy Road, Freetown, Sierra Leone
Kofi Annan Avenue, North Legon, Accra, Ghana
Publisher: Prof. Osman Sankoh (Mallam O.)
publisher@sl-writers-series.org
www.sl-writers-series.org

Acknowledgements

Our profound gratitude to God the Most High for the strength and courage he has given us to face this academic challenge.

Compiling this work of art has been one of the most momentous academic challenges we have ever faced as a team. Nevertheless, without the support, guidance, comments and encouragement of the following people, this piece would have never been completed and compiled. Thus, it is to them we owe our deepest appreciation:
- Dr Fatou Taqi for helping school going kids
- Morrison Jusu; our editor and mentor
- Joe Ahmed; our preview editor
- Mrs Hawa Saidu for tirelessly typing this great work
- Emily Fanday and Osman (Bullet) Dixon Kargbo for their motivation and consent to feature in our cover photo.

We would like to thank the Sierra Leonean Writers Series (SLWS) for their unprecedented support the opportunity given to us to expose our young talents.

Meet the Poets

Joseph Abdulai Jalloh also known as Jazz, was born in Freetown, Sierra Leone, attended Cockerill Preparatory and Junior Secondary school, later transferred to the Sierra Leone Grammar school. Took the West African Senior Secondary Certificate Examination and is about to be enrolled into university.

Anne-Marie Sankoh is a pupil of The International School Limited. She is in S.S.S 2 and is a school prefect.

Adeola Carew is a pupil of The International School Limited. Took the West African Senior Secondary Certificate Examination and is about to be enrolled into university.

Joe-Saymah Conteh is a Sierra Leonean born and raised who attended the J.T.Reffel Memorial School, The Sierra Leone Grammar School and currently is a student at the Fourah Bay College.

Saffyatu Ayomide Sesay, known to many as Saffy. She was born in Lagos, Nigeria. She attended the Becklyn Nursery and Preparatory School then went to the Annie Walsh Memorial School before switching to the Modern High School. She is in SSS4 at the moment.

Arthur Camiwor Cole, known commonly by friends and family as Camiwor or Cami. Born in Freetown. He attended the Modern Elementary School from daycare to Class 6 and later on went to the Sierra Leone Grammar School since JSS1. He is currently in SSS4.

Chinua Taylor-Pearce was born in 2000 in the USA. His family moved to Sierra Leone in 2010 where he has since resided and currently attends the Sierra Leone Grammar School.

Osman Dauda Bundu was born in Freetown. He attended the Sierra Leone Grammar School and he is currently pursuing a degree in Medicine at COMAHS, USL.

Amry Samuels born in Freetown Sierra Leone. Attended The Prince of Wales Junior Secondary, later furthered his senior schooling at The Sierra Leone Grammar School. He is currently at The Fourah Bay College studying engineering.

Table of Contents

Part 2 – Red Pages, 31-50

Part 3 – Yellow Pages, 52-58

Part 4 – Green Pages, 59-66

Chinua
    Our School's Glory Increases, 99

PART 1

White Pages

JOSEPH ABDULAI JALLOH (JAZZ)

FRITTERED

I picked up a piece of paper
I am just that naked blind fool
Who thinks poetry is an escape route
For letting out my pains
No it isn't
It is just that the ocean cleans the sand off the beach
With its rolling water
Yet makes it untidy
With its own filthiness
Keeping itself clean
Has the audacity of change
No one can haggle about its bizarreness
It weakens the mind from his drunkenness
Paving and painting a bright red margin line
Separating the heart from the mind.

Poetry is that perfect fire
That cleanses black dirty gold
Into the finest of substances
I want to carry myself
For letting this ailing ideas fall
Reaching the land from the mountains
Walking down with the commandments
I need to follow
Creating a living dead soul
Soaked in clay
Yet can't be subverted
Intrepid
Full of power and love
Courageous and newer lapsing

Poetry is that cage of life
That coaxes her wounds
Coating them with words as medicines
Words dressed in a nutshell
Full of fresh love
A field of open minds

Reaching the lost souls
Cleaning the depraved

Poetry is a cactus in the desert
Hope to the expiring soul
A perfect picture of desert with no blemish
Yet I've misused her powers

Drunken myself in her
Poetry is my outlet; or so I thought
It was just a way for me to push out my temporary rubbish
Conflicting ideas; internal battle being fought
I knew its worth, even though in recognition
I was sluggish

Hmmm, I finally dropped the sheet on the table
Finished reading a work done years back
I'm however a stronger being than I was
My poems reflected my personality
Showed what I felt
But not any more
I have evolved and changed for good

I'M A DAVID

Like Kendrick Lamar this is bigger than trying
I have got to face my Goliaths
Bring them down with no fear
Fearless I am fighting them
Fearless, I can't be defeated
Like David I've got sacred powers
I know I am a small stone
Holding unto a rock
Like a mighty statue in Babylon
I will bring them down
My armor and shield is the Lord of all
I am protected, secure and safe under his pavilion
I'll fight till the end
I can't be defeated
It's not in my blood
Goliath, be prepared
You think you can always belittle me?
In every aspect you try to pull me down
We've just started
At school or at home
You act as a bully
You take everything I put to test with
But know I'm coming soon
We are not done yet

PERFECT

Even when I'm gone it's like I never left
I'm the lion that rules, I always win, let's take a bet?
They are scared of my thunderous voice
They run into their shells and do according to my choice
I'm a fox; they all try to know my ways
Silent as I am, they come around just to study my ways
I'm getting too important these days,
Even my enemies whirl and cry
Just at the mention of my name they wish to die
I'm the shadow that covers their brightest lights
Yet without me they won't shine bright
I'm a devil that brings joy to their imagination
They won't be kings if I wasn't their greatest competition
They all know me, they hate me
Yet without me; Hell they are sound to be
I'm always around them when they go contrary
I open up and direct them to the way
I am just that perfect pain
That brings sunshine after the acidic rain
I am just super supreme
Of course I am no human being
I am just that perfect pain
That makes humanity a perfect gain
I am the ugly part
That started the sweet part
Without my ugliness, the rich will not remember the poor
Nor will saints walk to the sinner's door
Because of me you are insecure yet safe
O mankind! Be good to one another, don't play it safe
I guess you know who I am

OPTIMISM IN BLEAKNESS

Hi fantasy
Last night's dream was full of impossibilities
I asked for gold
You gave me coal
Maybe it is because my today is so bright
Anyways it is still useful
The burning mountain of volcanic ideas
Exploded and there's no clue it ever existed
I am not particularly scared to lose this fear
But the blur glass reflects nothing at all
That's where my fear lies
Losing everything
Even the few I have now
I turned to you for vision
What came out is good yet not satisfactory
Oliver Twist wants some more
You are supposed to be an impossible mission
But the greatest of inventions started from you
Leonardo Da Vinci is my witness

Mama always trusts in God
I do too
But that won't stop me from saying my mind
By the way the setting sun grew darker last night
From red to black
I've never seen it like that before
Why?
Anyways I am not afraid of adventures and impossible
missions
Joseph kept dreaming even when in jail
Why shouldn't I?

Joe told me all I've got is right now
Right now is all I need
That doesn't mean I'll stop dreaming anyways
It is a motivation for today
And only for today
I've got to accomplish it now
Life's traffic lights seem to be green always
Yet we seem to follow the red light instructions
Well in human heart red rules too
We all want to be the King Solomon of our time
I know we all can
But we all won't be
I just imagined the Garden of Eden, what it looked like
Having it all we are told that the journey of the unknown
started there
I fear tomorrow
Even though I have been told that
Over there's a greener side
I still fear to cross the bar
I am positive I'll not cross over until I have my print
On the book of life

SANDS OF TIME

Flash light of vision
Mother left
Water drips from my head
On to my jeans
Deep into my genes
One thing I remember
She always said
Leave your footprint on the sands of time

I started this journey on the beach
I didn't like the sun
It made the sand become hot coal to my bare feet
But then I never gave up
I was going to leave my footprints on the sands of time
I made sure my impressions were large enough
Large and deep enough for the blind to see and follow

My garage was full of papers and metals
Those are what I have to show I was alive
There are times when the sun got hotter
I felt I was on Venus
I prayed for sunset
It was sweet relief when the night drew near
But then it rained
My shelter was poor
I was wet
The good news I had enough water for the journey
As I moved along
I saw someone drowning
I saved her
My mother always helped me when I fell

So it was not strange for me to pull her out

She said her name was Sarah
She became my journey mate
Finally she let down her Berlin walls fall
At last our hearts collided
We created a bond
That could withstand a fall of Mount Everest
We planted a seed
It grew in a couple of days
The plant looked just like me
I taught him to leave his footprints on the sands of time
My feet became weary
I concluded I won't be able to leave my footprints on the whole beach
I made a stay

Just like my mother
I taught junior to always walk and work in day time
For the night will come and it shall be dark
He caged every bird that flew from my tongue
He carved the words into his heart
Leave your footprints on the sands of time
So deep that the waves can't wash them away
Please leave your footprints on the sands of time.

ARTHUR CAMIWOR COLE
JOE-SAYMAH-CONTEH
CHINNA TAYLOR-PEARCE
JOSEPH ABDULAI JALLOH (JAZZ)
CHRISPIN B. JOHNSON

TURTLE SHELL

I live life in perpetual fear
I always worry for my safety
And also for those that hold me dear
Who suggest I be more care free?

I see strangers as caution signs
I see danger as it always is
My actions are defined by narrow lines
As I stand atop the precipice

I carefully bury my heart in clay
In fear that it might be snatched away
Lips ever moving I always pray
That God protects me through each dangerous day

When people get close I pull away
My ability to trust is thinner than the needle's eye
I look for scenarios that help delay
My answer to questions that do not lie

Maybe it is the way I think
That separates me from the throng
That same thought has an unusual link
And makes me feel I'm always wrong

The flashlight dims inside my mind
As I wait patiently for help
Don't know those that are wicked from those that are kind
Through the ink from pen silently yelps

Life is worth living
So I take precautions in all I'm doing
I fear the dread of mankind's advice
Just like Judas to Christ, their words are full of lies

Even the few I choose to trust must
Have done the sacrifice of Abraham first
Even though I know we are dust
I stay away from hearts turned to frost

My life myself I'll have to live
So I live it as I believe
Just being free just being me
An army of white angels guide me

I like being a lone ranger
Always afraid of being in danger
I never let anyone in
I am my subject, prince and king

I walk through the valley alone
I insist on doing my work on my own
I am independent, strong and powerful
I am proud to put on this mantle

ARTHUR CAMIWOR COLE

THE POET

The poet! A man of natural talent
Very easy to set-off on a tangent
The mighty pen, the poet's own 'weapon'
The vast imagination; the poet's guiding beacon

The poet sees things as an aura of feeling
Turned into words; an understandable meaning
Love, hate, pain, happiness
All these emotions come from a natural intelligence

The poet sees nature as God's own beauty
And making nature known is his sole duty
The poet absorbs everything; land, sea and sky
He becomes one with nature; an unbreakable tie

The poet possesses an outstanding feature
From boy to man; a being so mature
The poet is able to use his wonderful insight
To write poems made up of will-power and might.

WHAT IF?

What if?
The world was still dark; no light to show the way or tell us the time of the day or help keep the demons at bay...
No spark

What if?
Life was nothing but an abyss; empty to the core
With nothing worth fighting for and everything dipped in blood and gore...
Yearning for a saving kiss

What if?
Men never evolved; relying on primal instincts, with visible ignorance of the increase of violent activities
That diminishes the presence of peace...murders left unresolved.

Sitting deep in my chasm of indecisiveness whilst biting my lip in thought and constructing scenarios
Of destroying those who reap without sowing what they keep...

What if?

ADEOLA CAREW

SILENT

Salone girls don't commit suicide
Our hearts might crack but they do not break
Love is real
As rank
As the next punch from our men
The next slap
As intangible as the never fulfilled promise of big houses
and fast cars from them

Fresh cuts over old wounds on my thigh
Blood stains on my towel
Dizzy spells
Moments of utter confusion
 I'm fading away
But resolutely suffering silently
"Cause Salone girls don't commit suicide"
We just bow out gracefully out of a losing battle
And wait for the award ceremony
Fighting for you to remember how you loved me when
we first met
The butterflies in your stomach
The panic of wanting to please
When I was the girl of your dreams
And stay.
That's losing a battle

MELANCHOLY

It's dark
I catnap
Alone in bed
Thinking
Maybe I'll write a song
About loneliness
About aloneness
Maybe heartbreak
About sadness
About darkness
Maybe tears
I'm lying alone
In bed
In my room
Wishing to be elsewhere
Curled up on the floor now
In this corner
Wishing to be elsewhere
Lying in bed
Forgotten

JOE-SAYMAH CONTEH

'POET'

I am a poet…well known for being as articulate as can be.. i can literally sugar coat the pain and suffering in hell…make a Christian swallow it together with his dead faith in three minutes

And if I am in the mood I could use these words to paint pictures of …
Sculpt the life, death and every other form of existence {whatever they might be} out of everything in every universe and beyond
Yet I can't say hi to her.

MY HEART RACES

My heart races perfectly in line with the heavy yet distant sound of mama fiercely doing handy at the back of the house and partially stops every time her phone rings.
My whole body shuts down in full support of my ears and that is not necessary because, even the deaf can hear her say "d dog no kam et, wetin mi n am de pas tidea nor lili."

CHINUA TAYLOR-PEARCE

PRESSURE

Like laminated paper or a picture in a frame,
Squeezed flat, no regrets about the way I came,
Scared of too many choices and also none at all,
Just a little too worried about a downfall.

But a child needs to grow up one day.
Display that they're ready to enter the fray.
But the fear and the worry, the pressure of it
Makes a youth yearn for days as a kid.

It's a gamble of course and I've seen it first hand.
But I know that capable is what I am
And I can take heart and have courage when I know
That my true abilities will in the end show.

With the pressure of life fear can sometimes take hold
But it is left to our faith to make sure we are bold.
Don't relax, but remember minds exaggerate.
You're stronger than you think, there's a will and a way.

WHAT'S A FRIEND?

What's a friend?
One that sticks with you to the end?
One on whom you depend?
One you'll always defend?

Sure, sometimes you'll fight
When they're wrong and you're right
But hesitate you might
Cause you know they're a light in your life.

A source of constant support
With a bond others can never thwart
A closeness that never aborts
Without which you'd be out of sorts.

So maybe I don't know
I've got theories but no proof to show
Some people just enter and go
And it's hard to know why they do so.

But when a real friendship is made
Over time you realize it's great
A true pal; that'll never betray
Is better than a million fakes.

WHAT I FEEL

I'm told to write about emotions
Share feelings that I myself don't understand
It's both awkward and absurd
But I'll do the best I can.

So I ask myself "what do I feel"?
Expecting a tidal wave
Of inner thoughts that might explain
The way people behave

No clear feeling stands out to me
I guess I'm a melting pot
Of worry, fear, stress and doubt
And confidence to even voice it out

In years of youth emotions are
Like bottles filled with volatile extracts
I say youths, but that might not change with age
Just based on how some elders act

So yes, I'll try and write a bit
On how I feel inside
But if it turns out that even I don't know
Please don't be too surprised.

DADS
For Dad

Too often we don't want to bother
To appreciate hardworking fathers
So friendly they're like older brothers
Yet all thanks goes straight to the mothers

Of course there are some absent dads
That doesn't mean we can't be glad
For those that work hard to provide
Their children with a decent life

They serve as role models for kids
They advise youths on how to live
Our fathers always have our backs
But still must suffer the media's wrath

So Dad, though more credit is due
And more thanks for the stress that you go through
For our child-father bond and the things you do
I just want to plainly say; thank you.

ANNMARIE SANKOH (S.A. HART)

SEE

Everyday
I hope and pray
That one of these days
I'll open my eyes
And see
Not through a haze of smoke
I wish the fog will rise
Not through the words they spoke
Saying I'll never summarize
The words I wrote
On that paper
They said hope was a lie
I was kidding my self; thinking I would ever survive
Through these battles, through these trails
Every inch of me suffocated; died
Counting my fingers hoping it will all add up someday
Someday it will mean something
But I still see nothing
A blank space laid out in front of me
Is that home?
I want to see
See past their blur
This myopic idiot wants to see
See the reason for the truth
And maybe, just maybe
See a brighter future
Where I can stay
I did what you said I could not do
I am what you said I could never be
And I am better than you ever thought I could be
That day I want to see

But I keep moving forward
For now
Through the dark
I tread an unknown path
Filled with mocking laughter
And mysterious gaze
I move forward
And pray
That one day
I will see
And feel
And laugh
Now I know
Now I see

PART 2

Red Pages

OSMAN BUNDU

BROKEN HEART

Pieces of broken heart lying on the floor
I sweep away my feelings but
Somehow, I don't seem to let go
I smile but you can see the freckles underneath
I try to eat but I just can't digest
The thought of you leaving me
I never thought this day would come
I never thought we would be happy as friends
I strive to make major steps towards the other side
Where the grass maybe greener but my feet miss you
My soul is still merged with yours and
I don't know how to set it free
I can't breathe as freely as I used to
I cried under the rain hoping it'll
Wash away the memories but to no avail
The cloud, like my feelings, never gets old as the rain drops
So do my tears, thinking about the time we had
The promises we made
I guess I can't rewrite history
It's clear you weren't meant for me
I hold onto the words you spoke as
I try to mend my broken heart

CHINUA TAYLOR- PEARCE

FORKS

I don't mean to be too depressing
But I'm sure you too find it distressing
That a basic decision
Made without precision
Can make life a great deal messier.

I mean, children, youths and teens
With much of life yet to be seen
Have to make huge choices
With immature voices
That in future may ruin their dreams!

Honestly, I never understood
Why anyone thinks that it's good
To have to choose paths
And suffer their wrath
But I guess that we have to and should.

So I guess I'll just have to assume
Though they may just lead us to our dooms
There are forks in the road
But at least now I know
Though I'll still always prefer a spoon!

POOR STATE

I walk past a homeless man sleeping
Not of riches but cigars he's probably dreaming
Doesn't care to progress; satiates basic needs
"We live in a poor state". Poor state indeed.

Check the streets at noon, school-boys in the town
Try to ask them, "Shouldn't you be at school now?"
Some don't care, some blame teachers, some are "going home
to read,"
Sure, "we live in a poor state." poor state indeed.

Clubs are full, parties raging, no one misses a "chilling"
If only we found all our work as fulfilling.
"It's the government's fault," but don't you concede?
Who created this "poor state?" for it's a poor state indeed.

Some grown men unemployed, happy to just drink wine
They don't dream of long term, just that dinner is fine
Drag us down like large weights, like parasites they feed
Maybe they are one cause of this "poor state", maybe

Our leaders relax and enjoy
Don't care 'bout the country they slowly destroy
No passion, no diligence, no integrity
Is this what we wanted when we became free?

SAFFYATU AYOMIDE SESAY

IMPERFECTION

I'm not perfect
I'm aware
My head is shaped like a tent
It can bring a building down, so beware

I'm not perfect
I've been told
My eyes like bulbs can be used to inspect
And kill a man's soul

I'm not perfect
Very true
My thighs are huge they can't be lifted (so don't try that when
we have sex)
Just like a pregnant woman who's overdue

I'm not perfect
Its okay
My lips are obviously crooked
Figured it out on my last birthday

I'm not perfect
That's fine
My arms can be used as a baseball bat
Got lots of words for it the last time
(you told me I'm imperfect so now why say you want me back
or somn' like that to end it here)

DARK DAYS

I'm a mess as I write this
Didn't want to show all my insecurities
Most of my dark days are because of these things

I broke down a month ago
They just had to point out my flaws
Nobody to run to
So I cried myself to sleep on the floor

This shit took over my life
Couldn't look in the mirror
Wanted to end it with a knife
There was so much horror

HUMANITY

They say the real ones are hard to find
I say the real ones don't exist
Humans go and kill each other's minds
My whole life, all I had was fake meats
I pray for the real ones to come
But I learnt you can't pray for what isn't alive
My mind and soul are not home
They are out looking for life
I don't want to sit with dead souls
I don't need hearts that are not kind
I am not into off kicks and charcoals
But in minds and brains that can grind
You hear them say "A1 since Day 1"
Yet they go out and confide in the graved ones
I spit at humanity
They lack spirit and unity
Why are you feeding me with decayed food?
Lucky that my immune system reeks of power
You're out killing fellow humans with good
Expecting me to motivate you with roars?
Your soul is what I loathe!

JOE-SAYMAH CONTEH

AS CURIOUS AS I AM

As curious as I am yesterday I fumbled in my girlfriend's purse
To my surprise I learnt she has been walking with three or
four other girls because
One I found a lip-gloss … sticky color sticks she carefully
applies to disguise those lips and make them look as if they
were mine
Two A sun glasses which has been programmed to show a
reflection of me in her eyes because her pupils contains
images of another guy … now I know why she always got
them on because she always got something to hide
Three A phone I never knew of
Four Shit my credit card
Five a packet of condoms …guess you already know what
that's for because she is like J.Cole on wet dreams "And I ain't
never did this before, no"
Six are those some contraceptive pills?
Seven I don't know what this is but I am pretty sure it is
harmful
Eight A Quran and a Bible
Nine my heart among a thousand others in a liquor bottle
labeled mine

AMRY SAMUELS

INTERCEPTION

Don't you dare do that again!
I can see you're over possessive
Don't think I'll play along!
I know you're a lion
But no need to find the alpha male
You're the walking boulder
I'm the noble lone wolf
Now, see your guts dissolve in gentility
Being consumed by self-brutality
Shocking! I recess...paired!

ARTHUR CAMIWOR COLE

EMOTIONAL ROLLER COASTER

Chaos laughs at my demise
A fool among the wise
A fool it turned me be
Drowning my dreams in the dark sea

Depression mocks my sanity
Taking away my capability
Letting me become vulnerable
Doubting my own competence like a traveler's fable

Nervousness is my downfall
An odd ball among all
A captain of my thinking skills
My intelligence it always kills

I cannot handle these stressful situations
That always evade my counter-stations
I look up to the heavens for a saviour
Oh mighty creator, let not me be a failure

ACTIONS

Never have I; looked a girl right in the eye
And tell her my feelings just to hear her sigh
And blush and give me bashful reply
That she felt the same way too

Never haven't I; sat alone in a room
Thinking about things to do in the afternoon
And waiting for the glow of the midnight full moon...
Wishing that you were true

But that's about change
Hey, Hi, Hello
I'm about to let these bottled up emotions explode
Hope you don't mind and I really don't care if you do
I won't sugar quote this with; Roses are Red and Violets are
Blue
I'll just be brutally honest with you.

But first I really got to pee

A LOVE POEM

When all I ever do
Is forever think of you
And wish you feel the same too
I write a love poem

When my heart skips a beat
On my cheeks I feel the heat
Of your love like I'd just been hit
I write a love poem

When I wanna see your face
When I try to pick the pace
On this meadow we currently race
I flip my lucky coin

You are forever in my heart
Till I die do we part
Keep this gift; my lucky dart
As I write you a love poem

ADEOLA CAREW

BLUE

Still can't remember when we first met
Bits and pieces all jumbled up
Yet I get surprisingly despondent
At the thought of getting up
One Monday morning
And you aren't there
We're part of each other now
And tomorrow
When life catches up with us
Time ravages our minds
Responsibility claims us
Know I'll still remember you
Making me laugh till my sides hurt
What we've got can't be destroyed
No matter how many times it's cut and shot
   Let's take two separate paths at the crossroads
So when we reach that light at the far end
Driving full throttle
Nerve endings overload
Sweat glands pouring
We'd have had all sort of incredible adventures to speak of
You'll say you once loved a poet
And I'll tell you about the stripper I might have married
If she was half as beautiful as you
Half as wild, half as hood
If she could have made me smile
   This thing I'm writing
It's not about me telling you what you already know
It's about me adding that I am never getting over this
This nonsensical, pointless feeling

This retarded, idiotic desecration of my heart
It's about me pretending to be a poet
So you'll spear me a glance
It's about me forsaking my pride as a pessimist for some
Shakespearean indulgence
It's about me pretending I've forgotten meeting you
When you were four
I was seven
I punched you in the face
Your beauty was too disturbing
You've gotten your pound of flesh since then
Every last bit and more

PART 3

Yellow Pages

JOSEPH ABDULAI JALLOH (JAZZ)

US

Ha! Ha! Ha!
Laughter from another room
I turned to see who it was
Of course it was her
Her voice is very unique
A perfect combination of fine notes
Seems to blast back
Whenever she speaks
It is very pleasing for the ears
I can still recall our last walk
Down the beach
I remember her blouse flew up when the fresh breeze blew
From the sea
Exposing her beautiful legs
I can still recall her pretty smile
She told me this
I'm a tree shade
A shade that can never be cut down

I smiled
I told her this
I'm a burning candle
A burning candle that can never be burnt down
She smiled
I still could feel her emotion
Her blissful eyes
Those brown shade pupils of her eyes
Her soft skin shinny and cool
She said she hated my guts
She's a shining star

She's got a heart of gold
She possess clear clean thoughts
Nothing fishy in her mind
She said I was handsome
I smiled and told her
I know already
Then she said
I hate men who know they are cute
I can't date a conscious man
So I replied
You are beautiful as a lily
She smiled and said thank you
So I said also
Cute people always love to be complemented
She finally agrees
I'll give you my soul
For eternity if you be my man
With joy I replied
Yes! Yes! Yes! I will
She turned to me with a frowned face
She asked
How can we succeed when we both are poor?
I replied
Success and I spoke yesterday
He told me, I don't need to be as bright as the sun to get to
him
All I need is hard work and dedication
She smiled
And said thank you
She swung her shining whiter dress
Against my dark black coat

Gave me a warm kiss
And spoke to my ears
I came with virgin lips
Now they are filled with messages of love
She ran to her blue car
And shouted
You are a very good actor
You've made me master my lines
Of course I should have known better
She has worked in the theatre for two weeks now
I was still in wonder land
When I heard a still but warm voice singing
He's very cute
Why don't you give him a try?
I smiled when I heard these words
Especially from her close friend

SONG UNHEARD OF

If I should write you a song
It will be full of natural tunes
Drums and other primitive instruments, I will use
I prefer to be old yet modern
The song will be full of love
Our children will line to express the final of it
Every stone will ring a bell
Serving as the new instrument designed by me
A glass will be by you
Filled with promises to quench your thirst
As you listen to me while I sing
The song will be like Nat King Cole
Your face in every flower
Your eyes in stars above
The end is yet to come
The dancers will walk on fire to the tune of music
The highest place I will place you to watch me sing for you
The lyrics will be quoted with love unseen
The earth will always remember this moment
I'll finally have the kiss you promised me years ago
The atmosphere will be of a nice fragrance
Its scent, much blessed than roses
The flowers I will give you will just match your purple dress
Designed for a goddess
And you are one
I will take you home after the song
To be mine forever
Dear beautiful love
I will sing you this everlasting song of love

HI IYE

I am Alloe Blac; go ahead and tell everybody I'm the
man. You're the Treasure Island and I'm Jimmy Hawkins full
of uncertainty about this journey.
One dream I have is to make this little Garden of Eden mine.
I know you'll be the perfect soil for my seeds.
The weather is uncertain rain or sunshine I hope to be your
umbrella; fit for every occasion. The jays can walk on air.
Gravity can't control us.
Waiting for your reply

PART 4

Green Pages

ARTHUR CAMIWOR COLE

BEAUTY

Beauty is a feature we all possess
Whether from love or gentle caress
Smooth as silk, sweet as honey
White as snow and equally sunny

Beauty is a gift meant to be adored
Wrapped in love a pure blessing from God
From an angle it can be a wild forest
When understood it's like an earth goddess

Beauty is a strong plane flying high
But when scorned it's hard to come by
It can be an influence too great to ignore
The root may be bad but good is the core

Beauty is found not in body but in soul
It can grow steadily like a newborn foal
Those who have beauty should use it well
Because it's from Heaven; certainly not from Hell

THE MOON

Through the silent night of God's own might
The moon shines its silvery light
Slicing through darkness a beam so bright
Hanging from the sky a wonderful sight

Dancing under the rays one finds happiness
The rays help reduce stress
The moon is a place of perfect rest
Forever soothing; seemingly the best

The moon's white face dotted with craters
Like the mesmerizing smiles of intriguing jokers
Compared to the stars, it is far greater
Even though the sun is much better

The light from the moon acts like a boon
Driving away darkness not a moment too soon
The white oval face; a protective cocoon
A natural night-light; the mystical moon

RAIN

Raindrops fall on the green earth
Heavens opening in their mighty wrath
Quenching the earth's scorching thirst
Moistening the soil and scattering dust
Raindrops fall from heaven above
The little drops make a mighty ocean
Lapping the shores in a wide curve
Increasing the strength of the tide's own motion

From the azure sky they fall down below
Cold to the bones right down to the marrow
Soaking the skin and healing dryness
Creating an intense feeling of calmness
Raindrops put the mind at ease
Bringing comfort by a thousand degrees
Patterning softly on the window pane
There is great joy for the drops of rain

CHINUA TAYLOR-PEARCE

DREAMS

Dreams are images in your mind
Of things in your future or left behind.
They are imagined and wished for by everyone:
Some give up on their dreams; others don't till they're done.
Dreams are your future, soon to be your past.
Some shall finish first; others will finish last.
Follow your dreams; give them your all
Because if you don't in the end you shall fall.

Other dreams happen when you are asleep.
Not until you lose consciousness on you they creep.
They can be anything; ahead or behind,
All lolling about inside your mind.
These dreams may come true, sometimes they don't.
You must try to achieve them, or else they won't.
Regardless of their kind, everyone has dreams.
Be careful with them; they're not always what they seem.

SUNSET

How long it's been since I've seen dear sunset
The contrast of beautiful orange and violet
Painted across the sky with free strokes
No noise to be heard, just the calm quiet
How can I stand to live without sunset?
Never seen the moon come out to play
Only to have the sun move hastily away
A fitting ending to a high stress day
Want to go somewhere I can see
The very beginning of the evening
No obstacle, smoke or city lights
To disturb the beauty of the night
For now I continue to miss
My own Aurora Borealis.

PART 5

Grey Pages

JOSEPH ABDULAI JALLOH (JAZZ)

BREEZE OF SILENCE

I feel the tension of something going wrong
I tried to know
But none could reply
Tell me! I exclaimed
But the silence still persisted
I checked the corner of my heart
Then I realized that they probably left
Before I came
Inside my heart was dark
Darker than the night
No light, no sound
Silent whispers of silence
I started roaring round like a lion in search of meat
Searching every corner
I prayed to find someone
But none showed up
Prayed all night
Searched all night

I'm all alone in this dark world
No helping hand
No one to call a friend
I am all alone
Dying for everything
Dying to find someone to talk to, someone to listen
Dying to be loved
Love never comes
The road is empty, dark and insecure
I walk this journey alone
Sometimes my eyes behold a figure
A reflection of my hopes

Figment of my imagination
No one is there
It just me and my broken bones
Fighting to be noticed
I've come to realize
No one will pass bye
Because in this world
It is difficult to meet someone who cares

DARK LIFE

My life has no light
People know
So they stay away
Goodness knows so she hates seeing me
Love understands, so she never finds me
Nothing good ever comes

My sight is gone
I can't see this earth people call beautiful
Everything I touch vanishes
I am heated
I hate knowing this
But I have to accept
Love can't find me
I am a beast to the world
No one wants me
No one cares about me

I am a neglected piece
A piece that only an expert can make perfect
I am searching for this expert
I have found none
I am still at war in search
I am broken
I am a roaming zombie
An empty room for destination
A place of rest only for the underdogs
Wiped out of the zone of first class

Even the last hope I have is taken away
Yes the only one I hang unto

She walked away
She says she loves me not
I hate myself for this
Myself, I trust not
I have no confidence in me
I am a "nobody"
A forgotten and destroyed piece of art

I look for the day I'll rise again
The day I'll love again
The day I'll set my eyes on success
When love shall finally find me at my hiding place
I will rejoice and grab that opportunity
To behold light again
To see the beauties of mother earth

Right now, it can't be possible because I'm blind
Blind to human love
Blind to make it right
Blind because I can't be trusted
O what a joy when I shall see again

MY FUTURE

My life hopes for a day of joy
A moment of peaceful reflections
A blessed moment with a sigh of success
Grabbing every opportunity as it knocks at my footstep
Will I ever receive that moment to grasp its joy?
To behold the light in this dark day
To reflect through my broken hours
When I sulk day and night to accept
The trounce of the day
Whichever it was
I kept my balance
I placed myself into shape
Creating a better me
My power of love is weakened
But my hope for a brighter success hangs on
Praying I live to love and learn again
Loving and learning to first accept
That my future won't be better
If I don't start to make it so now
Life is not a stainless clear glass
Containing pure water
But a clean contaminated running stream
That needs only a good purifier to make it better
Who's this purifier?
When will she come?
Will I still be alert to enjoy her?
Will she be able to separate the sediments from the pure substances?
I shall hope for her to come by
I still hope life will be better someday
Even though I know that life is a bed of roses

With thorns and sweet smelling fragrance
To endure and enjoy the timely beauty of life.

DISCARDED PIECE

I just broke a glass of water
It formed an ocean of waters in my heart
Bits of it fell from my eyes
Maybe a sign of regret
The flowing water quenched the burning desire in my heart
Now my heart is stone cold

I have lost the route of my journey
I don't know where to start
The destruction is too horrible to explain
The mountain of fortune I built years ago
Is now a low land of a desert
Birds can't nest there anymore
They've lost the melody to sing the songs of love

The only living creature I possessed
I killed with my own hands
A blue rag of dark hope
Hangs over me and won't go away
I blame myself for being too self-opinionated
They said it
I didn't listen
But whatever
I still move on
I wasn't the first to commit murder
I killed her love
And I killed mine too
There's still a lot to come
Life goes on

SAD HAPPINESS

I am too successful
To feel this hatred
For my precious soul
I can't even love my life
Love this stinking soul that none can love
Am I this whack?
Even a two month-old child resist me
What actually happed to the lovey dovy king?
Whose charm every soul loves to behold
His total dedication to gain success
I guess I can never go back to the past
Never accelerate my life to the future
So I'll live my life the way I have it now
These things, I just can't change
Forget about relationships because I won't get one; love sucks
But then I met Olive
She is a Jonah
Waiting to be swallowed by the fish before she obeys
She's trapped in her own emotions
Her heart now tormented
Slowly turning into a rock
Of course she is vulnerable
To the sick and dying world
The world of hash weather
She sees her dreams
Slowly meeting a dead end
How soon will she get there?
Life is unfair
She is lost in lust
She can't love
Maybe if the sun turns black

And remains black
She can wear the perfect white gown for her wedding
Serving as the light to her world
If only her life could dissolve
Its blueness into the sea
Then she can see and express
The redness in her
Hopefully I will be that green light
To start her journey of love.

MY PIANO

I don't understand my piano anymore
It seems to be playing noise
Instead of music
My audience are tired of listening to me
They've left, gone to those who play it well
My waist is tired of sitting
My feet are tired of standing
My eyes are tired of watching the music score
My teacher is tired of correcting me
I give up
I won't play anymore
From now on, I'll play to please me

I took a break
Washed my eyes
The scales fell off
I then realized I was looking at the wrong score
I changed the score
Played it like I saw it
Pleased my own soul, my ears
This is my music
I don't care what they feel
I will play it from now on, to please me

PANTING HARD

Hidden in the walls of the prison cell
Cameras' flashing lights
Suddenly sounds of motion in my ward
Fear overcame me

Losing my faith
Waiting for fate to act
I don't know you
Stop chasing me
I'm in a dark glooming doorway
Backed with a blocked mindset
Can't see the open space
Batimius can see perfectly in comparison
But really they stabbed me too hard
For being too gullible

My eyes yearned for light
Sounded by eternal darkness
Fighting for my sense of sight
The darkness closed in
Looking for a way
Out of my charm of despair
I'm lost in my nightmares

Nothing seems to guide me
Out of this darkness rose a dark one
My demons destroyed my train of thoughts
Blinding my sense of judgement
And direction
A lost soul lost

A lost soul in a lost world
Lost my direction
My ability to perceive
My ability to believe
Still yearning for the light
Lost everything I had
And all that I loved
You saw to that
I thought you were human
You broke my red skin
Tore down the walls that protected it
And left me lost
Lost in realms

Liquor bottle in my hand
The redline is sure
My imperfection holds on
Who cares; death is sure
Bubbled emotions laying down on the floor
Even my skin is bleeding
My heart of course; a test tube of blood
Crushed life; crushed me
The dead living beings are angry
They rent their white robes and walked away
They are not here to take
So I feel a bit secure
Filling in the spaces
Blue lights in the delivery room
Another me in the making?
I guess so
There's light all along
Just the decade living being disturbed me
From feeling it

I woke up
Nasty dream!
Cut! Cut! Cut!
Nice, I love it
Genius

FRUIT OF THE SOUL

I don't want to say this
But it is a log in my brutal imagination
I am just this perfect ripe fruit
That looks perfectly outside
Juicy and mature
Accepted as mature for eating
But once tasted, I am sour
I have been baked so hard by the sun
That I look ready
I am even scared to tell them
That my land is still a virgin
Free the waters and water my soul
I have been looking for proper fertilizer
To maintain my organic factors

But the problem with the farmers is, they think
I actually don't need a fertilizer
I want to break this bound
I want to know how it feels like
To be involved with fertilizers
It is the sole dream of every plan
To be rich in what makes him produce
I actually don't want to produce

I don't feel ready
But I want to feel the fertilizer
I want to believe I've got it
That producing sweet fruits will be the best
The only decision I can take currently
Is to learn by watching
But that's archaic

A HEART'S CONVERSATION

Your words are like stray bullets
Touching where they are not sent
They're like the broken arrows piercing my soul
I am now a bleeding living being
Waiting for death to unleash its power over me
Every soul of Eve's kind seems to be a curse to me
As long as I plan to be the Adam of their life
I regret trying, but every time I don't
It is like I'm loving the life of a futile plant
The green soil is always smiling
I wish I were theirs'
Yet I trample upon them daily
They spring up the next rainy day
Resting disturbs them
Will you help me?
I am pissed off
I threw the notes into the drawer
I heard my door opened
Bonny and Banny were already home
They were having a discussion
Hey she's here
Kiss her he replied
Nah I can't
She's a bull dog
At the same time a brave female generic dog
She's rude, protective yet free
Wow! So what are you trying to say?
That she's a snake friend?
Of course!
A perfect viper
She lies low and fittingly to the brown dust

She comes as a perfect friend
At the end she turns into the vampire
That has no mercy
Hmmm, you don't say?
Well that's what it is
I can't date her and I would advise you to do likewise
Nice piece of advice
He replied
But I know how to deal with such a bitch
I'm a lion for hot ladies
Also a chameleon for the quick game changers
Can be rude as a female dog on heat
Yet calm as a cat awaiting a rat
Just obscure our conversation

Banny is right every soul of Eve sucks
I finally went inside to continue writing the notes
The one to the perfect soul I've not yet met

SAFFYATU AYOMIDE SESAY

LETHAL CONFESSION

A part of my soul is very bitter
My head will fall off if I go a day without thinking of ways to
get you slaughtered
Seeing you turns my heart into a black hole
I need you to go
Depart from my life and into any of the unknown alternate
universes
That voice of yours strengthens the poison you deposited into
my cracked soul
Only if you knew how much I want this venom in me to
destroy your soul
Like grade-A cancer would do
To drag you to hell by your head
I want you to feel every ounce of pain Jesus felt
Because of reasons that are vain
Whore! You've ruined my mind
Destroyed my saintly home
I want you to feel like a rejected citizen in your own home
Stop with the pretense
Go outside and kill yourself
I just need you to die
So I can sleep with a smile

ADEOLA CAREW

HAUNTED

Running on the forest floor
Trees toppling high kissing the heavens
Keep me, save me
Excruciating pain in her thigh
Hands caked with mud and blood
But...
Fast, fast, faster still
Till exhaustion overcomes
And she stumbles.

ARTHUR CAMIWOR COLE

REVENGE

My mind was destroyed
My will-power gone
My enemy was employed
To make sure I was burned

I was chased by the beast
The world a moving blur
I was chased into the mist
My face marked by a claw

Loving was no longer an option
My hate was bought at an auction
You slyly stole my soul
You left me to die in a dark hole

I begged you for death
You smiled and gave me crystal meth
The tables have now been turned
Tonight I'll see you burn

VENGEANCE

Dark clouds overhead
Lying lonely in my bed
Where is my saviour?
Where is my friend?

I thought I had it all
I thought you'd hear my call
But boy I was wrong
Now banging my head against the wall

Where exactly where you?
When I mostly needed you?
No one's home now
Hope you enjoy the dark view

Now here you lay
Tossed into the fray
I have only hatred
You will die today

DARK OATH

The Dark cloud is approaching
Becoming very unbecoming
An indication of my change
To test my anger's range

My eyes see fire-red
Burning words once read
Words that cut deep in my heart
Destroying love we shared on the yacht

I am devoid of emotions except one
Emotion I discovered when you've had your fun
Emotion that's the cause of my destruction
Emotion I thought was lost with evolution

You were the cause of my downfall
Savageness sent me to Hell's dark hall
I promise you would join me soon
And forever will you sleep in a fiery cocoon

HELL'S DEMON

If my heart was any darker
If I was death's apprentice reaper
Etched in your memory as a nightmare
I will forever haunt you my dear

As your last days alive draw near
Be ready to face your worst fear
Screams are null; no matter how loud
I will come in the night as a dark cloud

Down the shadowy depths of hell
Down to where no man can tell
The horrors that await every mortal
Who dare enter the forbidden portal

PART 6

Purple Pages

JOSEPH ABDULAI JALLOH (JAZZ)

TEST OF TIME

Through 170 years, our Grammar School has been glorious
Through challenges, wars and sickness, we're victorious
We rise up, shake off the dust and pursue
Always full of determination
Endeavoring to do things to perfection
First of her kind in this region
Is dedicated to give this land quality education
For present and future generations
She started as a small institution
Given to us by a humble religion
The missionaries taught us to always give God devotion

Upon that ancient site; Regent Square, started the vision
Of service, excellence and dedication
From then on, first class became our possession
Success became our passion
From that single great building to our Murray Town Mansion
Proprietor, old boys, parents, staff and pupils work in one
great union
One happy family heading in the same direction
To achieve the prize of the upward call and be the best in this
nation and region

At school and work we have the best reputation
Our old boys are our admiration
They show generosity through donations, scholarship and
motivation
We work hard to get the best in all occupations
We are always prepared like the first Freetown Troops
To be the best of schools; always at the top

God bless our Grammar School!
On this septendencintary (170 years of existence 1845 - 2015)

CHINUA TAYLOR-PEARCE

OUR SCHOOL'S GLORY INCREASES

Our grand old school, her glory now
Shall soon increase fourfold
Her glory, she wears like a crown
The best, wondrous and old
Our school has always been the best
She is a cut above the rest
She has passed every single test
Let everyone be told.

Now with a brand new building
We will stay at the top
As this great institution grows
Her wonder never stops
As we go through another phase
Passing through with amazing grace
Surprise on every single face
Looking at the new crop.

As the Reverend Thomas Peyton
Created this great school
At its first site at Regent Square
And made its lawful rules
I'm sure that he would look with pride
To see this, his eyes would go wide
He'd say to us all and with him we'd cry
GOD BLESS OUR GRAMMAR SCHOOL!

www.ingramcontent.com/pod-product-compliance
Lightning Source LLC
Chambersburg PA
CBHW031324040426
42443CB00005B/211